FRIENDS
OF ACPL

**DO NOT REMOVE
CARDS FROM POCKET**

SPORTS GREAT
STEFFI
GRAF

—Sports Great Books —

Sports Great Jim Abbott
(ISBN 0-89490-395-0)

Sports Great Troy Aikman
(ISBN 0-89490-593-7)

Sports Great Charles Barkley
(ISBN 0-89490-386-1)

Sports Great Larry Bird
(ISBN 0-89490-368-3)

Sports Great Barry Bonds
(ISBN 0-89490-595-3)

Sports Great Bobby Bonilla
(ISBN 0-89490-417-5)

Sports Great Will Clark
(ISBN 0-89490-390-X)

Sports Great Roger Clemens
(ISBN 0-89490-284-9)

Sports Great John Elway
(ISBN 0-89490-282-2)

Sports Great Patrick Ewing
(ISBN 0-89490-369-1)

Sports Great Steffi Graf
(ISBN 0-89490-597-X)

Sports Great Orel Hershiser
(ISBN 0-89490-389-6)

Sports Great Bo Jackson
(ISBN 0-89490-281-4)

**Sports Great Magic Johnson
(Revised and Expanded)**
(ISBN 0-89490-348-9)

Sports Great Michael Jordan
(ISBN 0-89490-370-5)

Sports Great Mario Lemieux
(ISBN 0-89490-596-1)

Sports Great Karl Malone
(ISBN 0-89490-599-6)

Sports Great Kevin Mitchell
(ISBN 0-89490-388-8)

Sports Great Joe Montana
(ISBN 0-89490-371-3)

Sports Great Hakeem Olajuwon
(ISBN 0-89490-372-1)

Sports Great Shaquille O'Neal
(ISBN 0-89490-594-5)

Sports Great Kirby Puckett
(ISBN 0-89490-392-6)

Sports Great Jerry Rice
(ISBN 0-89490-419-1)

Sports Great Cal Ripken, Jr.
(ISBN 0-89490-387-X)

Sports Great David Robinson
(ISBN 0-89490-373-X)

Sports Great Nolan Ryan
(ISBN 0-89490-394-2)

Sports Great Barry Sanders
(ISBN 0-89490-418-3)

Sports Great John Stockton
(ISBN 0-89490-598-8)

Sports Great Darryl Strawberry
(ISBN 0-89490-291-1)

Sports Great Isiah Thomas
(ISBN 0-89490-374-8)

Sports Great Herschel Walker
(ISBN 0-89490-207-5)

SPORTS GREAT
STEFFI
GRAF

—Sports Great Books—

Ron Knapp

ENSLOW PUBLISHERS, INC.

44 Fadem Road	P.O. Box 38
Box 699	Aldershot
Springfield, N.J. 07081	Hants GU12 6BP
U.S.A.	U.K.

Library of Congress Cataloging-in-Publication Data

Knapp, Ron.
Sports great Steffi Graf / Ron Knapp.
     p. cm. — (Sports great books)
  Includes index.
  ISBN 0-89490-597-X
    1. Graf, Stephanie, 1969– —Juvenile literature. 2. Tennis
players—Germany—Biography—Juvenile literature. [1. Graf, Stephanie, 1969– .
2. Tennis players. 3. Women—Biography.] I. Title. II. Series.
GV994.G7K63 1995
796.342'092—dc20
[B]
                                              94-30538
                                                 CIP
                                                      AC

Printed in the United States of America

10 9 8 7 6 5 4 3 2 1

Photo Credits: Michael Baz, pp. 8, 10, 13, 14, 16, 18, 21, 25, 27, 31, 33, 37, 39, 40, 44, 48, 51, 53, 59.

Cover Photo: Michael Baz

Contents

Chapter 1

Nobody in tennis history ever had a year like the one Steffi Graf had in 1988.

At Wimbledon, she buried her first seven opponents. None of the matches took longer than an hour. At last, in the finals, she faced Martina Navratilova, the legendary athlete who was going for her ninth Wimbledon singles title.

Graf jumped to a 5–3 lead. She only needed one more game to take the first set. But then Martina went to work, winning the next six games. That gave her a 7–5 first set victory and a 2–0 lead in the second. Steffi could almost feel the match slipping away, and she was angry. Was she about to blow the most important match of her life? Not her!

Graf slammed a ball into the backstop and glared at Navratilova. Come on, she seemed to be saying, give me your best shot. Martina served the ball to Steffi's right and she blasted it back past her. Minutes later she had broken the champ's serve and won her first game of the second set.

In the next game, Steffi was all over the court. When Martina lobbed the ball over her head, she raced back to slap

Steffi Graf is one of the top tennis players in the world.

it over the net. With her opponent all the way back behind the baseline, Martina dropped a soft shot just over the net. But Steffi raced up, hit the ball, and won the point. Soon the game was hers and the set was tied, 2–2.

Good tennis players always expect to win when they're serving. Navratilova was one of the best, and yet she never served another win that day. She was broken seven times in a row. Steffi won twelve of the last thirteen games. She took the last two sets—and the prestigious Wimbledon championship—6–2, 6–1.

"I got blown out," Martina said. "Steffi's speed—her incredible spring—is her biggest weapon. She's so quick off the mark." Navratilova felt as though the championship trophy had been ripped out of her hands.

When Steffi got the trophy in her own hands, she acted as if she didn't know what to do with it. An official had to explain that it was customary for the winner to hold the trophy over her head, displaying it for the crowd. It was Graf's first win at Wimbledon, and she wasn't sure how it was done.

All the same, she'd already had some experience winning big tournaments. The top four—the Australian Open, French Open, Wimbledon, and United States Open—are known as Grand Slam events. Steffi had won the 1988 Australian Open in January by beating Chris Evert, 6–1, 7–6. Then in June, she'd shut out Natalia Zvereva, 6–0, 6–0, to take the French Open. It was the first time since 1911 that the winner hadn't let her opponent win a single game. The match was over in just thirty-two minutes. Some of the fans were disappointed—they had wanted to see a long, exciting match. Graf apologized, "I'm very sorry it was so fast." She liked to win, but she also liked her matches to be interesting. "I can get bored if things go too easily," she said. "I'm not happy with

In 1988, Steffi upset Martina Navratilova in the Wimbledon final, breaking Martina's six-year winning streak.

my opponent then. . . . Some of my matches don't last as long as signing autographs or giving interviews."

After Wimbledon, there was only one major event left—the U.S. Open. If Steffi won there, she would have a Grand Slam, a clean sweep of the year's most important championships. Only two women had ever won a Grand Slam—Maureen Connolly in 1953 and Margaret Court in 1970. Graf was anxious to join them. "It is strange that Chris and Martina could not win the Grand Slam," she said. "They were so dominant and won so easily. Now I am nineteen and on the way to doing it. The Slam is very important. You can win the U.S. Open ten times, but it's not like winning the Slam."

Steffi made it to the finals of the U.S. Open, but her opponent wouldn't be Navratilova or Evert. Martina had lost in the quarterfinals to Zina Garrison, and Chris had to leave her semifinal match because of a stomach virus. Graf's opponent for the championship would be Argentina's Gabriela Sabatini, the only player who had beaten her twice in 1988.

At first, Steffi seemed to have trouble judging balls in the swirling winds of the National Tennis Center in New York City. Sabatini kept hitting long shots with lots of topspin that kept her at the baseline. But Graf was still able to take the first set, 6–3.

Then Gabriela got hot. She broke Steffi in the fourth game. At this point, Graf seemed to have trouble even keeping the ball in the court. "In the second set, I was not so tough," she admitted. Sabatini won, 6–3, and the match was tied. The crowd of 21,000 cheered. Most of them wanted to see somebody finally beat Steffi. "I knew she had to be nervous. . . ." Gabriela said. "I played like I did against her in the last matches. I hit deep balls. That bothers her very much."

But Sabatini ran out of steam. Graf won the first game of the third set on her own serve. She won the next, too, even though Sabatini was serving. And she didn't let Gabriela win a single point—it was a love game. Four games later Sabatini was broken again. She lost the last point of that game by hitting two straight serves into the net—a double fault. It made the score 5–1. Graf needed just one more game.

Sabatini was winded. She knew she was through. To finish her off on match point, Steffi drilled over a backhand crosscourt shot that almost knocked the racket out of Gabriela's hand. Graf had won, 6–3, 3–6, 6–1. She had the U.S. Open. And, more important, she had the Grand Slam!

Steffi threw her racket into the air and raced for the stands. She hugged her parents, Peter and Heidi, and her brother Michael. Then she went back to receive her trophy. Besides that, she was awarded a gold bracelet with four diamonds, one for each of her Grand Slam victories. She was also presented a $275,000 check for winning the U.S. Open. But that didn't seem very important—after all, she had already won more than a million dollars in 1988. What mattered most was the Grand Slam.

And Graf wasn't finished yet. After a brief rest at her home in Bruhl, Germany, she headed to Seoul, South Korea, and the Olympic Games. For the first time in many years, tennis would be an official event.

In her early matches Steffi seemed tired, and it looked as though she might be beaten. But by the semifinals, she was once again playing almost flawless tennis. She whipped Garrison, 6–2, 6–0.

In the finals, her opponent was once again Sabatini. This time it wasn't even close. Steffi's solid shots were sharper than ever, and she won, 6–3, 6–3. She had a gold medal to go with her Grand Slam! Nobody before had ever done that.

Graf smiled and said she could relax: "Now there's nothing else that people can tell me I have to do."

Graf proudly displays her U.S. Open trophy.

Graf became the first tennis player to win both the Grand Slam and an Olympic gold medal.

Chapter 2

Stephanie Maria Graf was the first child of Peter and Heidi Graf. She was born on June 14, 1969, in Mannheim, Germany (formerly West Germany), a large city with many factories. Their home was just forty miles northeast of France.

Peter was a partner in an automobile dealership, and also sold insurance. But in his spare time, he loved to play soccer and tennis. Mr. Graf was a tough competitor, and he always played to win. Many times he tore leg muscles on the soccer field. On the tennis court, he was good enough to be the top-ranked player at the local club.

Heidi Graf also enjoyed tennis. When she and her husband played, they usually took Steffi and her little brother, Michael, to watch. The children enjoyed being at the club, but Steffi soon got tired of just watching. When she was three years old she began saying, "Oh, Papa, I want to play like you." At first Peter laughed at his daughter's idea. After all, she wasn't even big enough to hold a full-sized tennis racket. But Steffi was determined.

Peter said afterward, "Every day there she was, waiting for

Steffi races for a backhand return. From the age of four, she showed great enthusiasm for tennis.

me at the door. 'Please play with me, Papa.' Not four years old. She pestered me and pestered me. I believed maybe she only wanted to play because she loved me and wanted to be like me."

But Mr. Graf finally gave in. He sawed off the handle of one of his rackets so Steffi could hold it. She wasn't big enough for a real court, so they practiced inside the house. "We played in the living room and also in a big hobby room with billiards and things like this," she said. "We put two chairs up and we played over them."

At first the game wasn't easy for the little girl. "We broke a lot of lamps. Many," said Mrs. Graf. "Then we moved everything downstairs into a playroom."

By the time she was four years old, Steffi could hit the ball back to her father over the chairs. He decided to challenge her. "If she could get the ball back ten times, I would reward her with a breadstick," he said. Soon the little girl had eaten most of the breadsticks in the house. Then Mr. Graf made it tougher. He offered her a glass of soda pop each time she returned the ball fifteen times in a row. It wasn't long before Steffi was enjoying lots of pop.

"Then I told her if she could get it back twenty-five times, we would make a party with ice cream and hot strawberries," said Mr. Graf. Soon even twenty-five returns was easy for Steffi, so her father made it harder. As soon as she had twenty-four, he would give her a tough shot that was impossible to return. "You can't have parties all the time," he said.

Mr. Graf soon realized that his daughter had the potential to be a very good player. "The evidence of her talent became very strong," he said. "Unlike the other children, she did not hit the ball and then look all around at other things. She was always watching the ball until it was not in play anymore."

As a young girl, Steffi learned tennis by playing in the German Tennis Federation. There she first met Boris Becker, who would also become a world champion tennis player.

Steffi loved the game, and loved spending time with her father. "It was really much fun," she said, "But it was always me and my father. . . ."

When she was five, she played her first game on a real court. She didn't think it was any harder than playing in the basement at home. She began competing against children her own age—and older. When she was six, she won her first tournament, a juniors event for eight-year-olds and younger.

Peter Graf sold the auto dealership in Mannheim and quit selling insurance. He moved his family to Bruhl, a smaller town just to the south. There he and his wife opened their own tennis club. The new arrangement gave him more time to practice with Steffi. She also began playing in the German Tennis Federation's program at nearby Liemen. That's where she first met eight-year-old Boris Becker, a little blond-haired boy a year older than she was. "She could hit it," Becker remembered years later when they were both Wimbledon champions. "I was not as good as the good boys, and so I had to practice with the best girls. She was the best girl."

As she grew older, Steffi never stopped loving tennis and practicing. "All I want to do is play good tennis and have fun," she said years later. "I want so much to hit it hard—and have it go in."

Some parents said Mr. Graf was ruining his daughter's life by forcing her to play tennis all the time. "Steffi works much harder than the other girls because she wants to," he said. "I have never pushed her. That is why she is so good. How long we play has always depended on how long she wants to play." When her father set a time for practice, she almost always showed up early.

It seemed to some of her classmates that Steffi wasn't interested in anything except tennis. Once she was invited to a friend's birthday party, but said she couldn't go because she didn't want to miss tennis practice. Mr. Graf said that wasn't right. "I made her go to the party."

Even though she was still very young, Steffi was earning a reputation in Germany as a fine tennis player. Isabel Cueto, another young German player, watched Steffi compete in a tournament when she was eight. "I was nine," she said. "My parents and I couldn't believe it. They knew I would need some more lessons."

In 1981, Steffi won the German fourteen-and-under championship, as well as the eighteen-and-under title. She was still only twelve. The next year she won the European tournament for twelve-and-under players. By then there were only eleven female players who were nationally ranked higher than Steffi—and they were all adults.

Mr. Graf decided it was time for Steffi to start competing against the best women athletes in the world. Until then, all of her tournaments had been amateur events. That meant that she only won trophies or plaques, not prize money. But for professional athletes, tennis is a full-time job—they want more than just trophies.

Most professional sports are still closed to women, but not tennis. Its female stars are the highest paid women athletes in the world. When Steffi was a young girl just learning to play, women like Martina Navratilova and Chris Evert were earning hundreds of thousands of dollars winning professional tennis tournaments.

In 1982, when she was only thirteen, Steffi became a professional. She joined the women's tennis circuit. That meant she would be traveling around the world to tournaments in places like the United States, France, Australia, and Great Britain. It would be impossible for her to attend school in Bruhl.

Navratilova thought Steffi was rushing her career. In a

From the time she turned professional at the age of thirteen, Steffi has been a serious, focused player.

letter to her future opponent, Martina told Steffi she should stay in school and enjoy being a kid. There would be plenty of time to play tennis after she graduated. But Steffi and her father didn't want to wait. They figured she was already good enough to compete against players like Martina. They were anxious to see how well she would do. They were also anxious to see how much money she could earn as a professional.

And so, even though she was only in eighth grade, Steffi quit school. Her father hired a tutor to teach her as they traveled around the world, but it wasn't the same. Steffi was the only student in this class, and she only had time for her studies when she wasn't busy with tennis.

At first she wasn't a big winner on the professional tour. She was ranked the 214th best player in the world by the Women's Tennis Association. In her first year, she didn't win any tournaments at all. Usually she was lucky to win one match before losing the next one and being eliminated.

Some of the older players weren't much impressed with the young German girl. Tracy Austin was tied, 4–4, with Steffi at a match in Filderstadt, Germany, before she got hot and wiped her out, 6–4, 6–0. The German reporters asked Austin what she thought of Graf. Not much. Tracy said, "There are a hundred like her back in the States."

In December 1983 at the Australian Open, Steffi fell, tearing the tendons in her hand. Playing despite the injury, she lost the first set of her opening match, 6–1. By then her thumb hurt so badly she had to give up. She went home to Germany to let it heal.

Many fans wondered if Steffi had made a mistake by turning professional. In her first year, she had won no tournaments and hardly any money. Even when she was winning she never seemed to be having any fun. On the court she was always serious. Usually she looked angry. Steffi thought that was a silly thing to worry about. "I like to laugh," she said. "But on the court, it is my work. I try to smile, but it is so difficult. I concentrate on the ball, not on my face."

Whether she was smiling or not, people wondered how long she could last on the pro circuit. How much longer could Steffi and her parents and her tutor afford to travel to tournaments all around the world? And beyond that, should a fourteen-year-old girl be trying to make a living playing tennis? Maybe Navratilova had been right. Maybe Steffi should have stayed home in Bruhl. Wouldn't she have been happier just going to school and spending time with friends her own age?

But Steffi had no doubts. "The thing that girls want to do is talk about boys, boys, boys," she said. "And go to discos. Those are not what I want to do at the moment." All Steffi Graf wanted to do was play tennis.

Chapter 3

As soon as the thumb healed, Steffi Graf was back on the court. Early in 1984 she began winning more regularly. She made it to the final eight of the German Open, and then didn't lose until the finals of a tournament in Filderstadt, Germany.

But the toughest, most prestigious events in professional tennis are the Grand Slam tournaments—the Australian Open, French Open, Wimbledon, and U.S. Open. In May, Steffi didn't lose until the third round at the French. A few weeks later she made it to the fourth round at Wimbledon. She and her father were beginning to believe that she really belonged on the women's tour. They dreamed of the days when they hoped she would be winning Grand Slam tournaments.

In August of 1984, the world's greatest athletes gathered in Los Angeles for the Summer Olympics. Michael Gross, the great German swimmer, was there. So were the American track stars, Carl Lewis and Evelyn Ashford. Mary Lou Retton was leading the United States gymnastics team.

With all the superstars in town, hardly anybody paid attention to the fifteen-year-old German tennis player from

Steffi gets ready to rush the net.

Bruhl. But Steffi was also one of the competitors. For the first time in sixty years, tennis would be part of the Olympics—not as an official event, but as a "demonstration" sport. The world's best players weren't there because it was limited to athletes twenty-one and younger.

Even though she was the youngest female competitor, the 1984 Olympics proved to be a great opportunity for Steffi to demonstrate her talent. With thousands watching from the stands and millions more on television, she won her first four matches to earn a spot in the finals against Yugoslavia's Sabrina Goles. It was a chance to win her first important tournament and earn an honorary Olympic gold medal. Steffi made the most of it by beating Goles, 1–6, 6–3, 6–4.

The Olympic victory, of course, was the highlight of the year for Graf. There was no prize money involved, but she was confident that she would soon be winning that in professional tournaments. However, back on the pro circuit, she was again competing against veteran women players. There were no more championships in 1984.

In January 1985, Steffi was ranked twenty-second in the world by the Women's Tennis Association. That was 192 spots above her first ranking, less than two years earlier. She continued to move up by winning most of her matches. She made it to the finals of the German Open, as well as tournaments in Mahwah, New Jersey, and Fort Lauderdale, Florida. She had her best performances yet at the French Open and Wimbledon, finishing in the final sixteen of both events.

Then on a hot September day in the quarterfinals of the U.S. Open, Steffi played what was up until then the greatest match of her life. With the temperature around a hundred degrees, she faced Pam Shriver, the third-highest-ranked player in the world. The two women battled to a 6–6 tie in the opening set before Steffi finally took it in the tiebreaker. But

During her first few years on the tour, Steffi suffered frustrating losses to veteran players such as Martina Navratilova and Pam Shriver.

Shriver won the second set in another tiebreaker, and jumped to a 5–3 lead in the third. If she took just one more game, she would win. But Graf got tough, battling back to tie the set 6–6. Once again the women had to go to a tiebreaker. Steffi won, 7–4, and the match was hers.

The Shriver-Graf quarterfinal is still talked about as one of the most exciting tennis matches ever played. It was the first time three consecutive women's sets had been decided by tiebreakers. "It was such an unbelievably close match," Graf said. "In the first set tiebreaker she was up 3–0 and serving, and I thought this set was away. And I got it! Then the next set I was up 4–1 in the tiebreaker. And I lost it! Finally, in the third set I was 4–1 down and I thought, 'Aw, I let it slip away.' And again I got it. It was just unbelievable." After the two hour and forty-five minute match, both players were drenched in sweat. Shriver sobbed in disappointment as the crowd cheered Steffi.

In her next match at the U.S. Open, Graf was destroyed by Martina Navratilova, then the Number One player in the world. Steffi wasn't ready to win the Grand Slam tournaments quite yet.

She also wasn't ready to face some of the pressure and disappointment that comes in big time tennis. Two months after their great match at the U.S. Open, Graf and Shriver met again, this time in Filderstadt. Shriver upset Steffi by waving at her bad shots and sticking out her tongue. Graf was angry that Pam wasn't penalized for her poor sportsmanship. She stormed off the court and promised she would never go back to that city.

At the finals of the 1985 Maybelline Classic in Fort Lauderdale, Steffi was defeated by Navratilova. Instead of waiting for trophies and checks to be presented, she ran off the court to the locker room. The fans in the stands and watching on television thought she was behaving like a spoiled brat. Her father chased after her, saying, "Come, come, come," and finally she returned to the court. But as soon as she received her second-place check for $14,500, she ran off again—even before Navratilova got her check. The headline in one paper read, "Graf Takes 2nd-Place Cash, Runs."

Again some people wondered if Steffi belonged on the pro circuit. Maybe she was just a temperamental youngster being forced to play tennis hour after hour by her ambitious father. Steffi apologized for her temper tantrum in Florida, but she was tired of people criticizing Peter Graf. "My father is only trying to do the best for me," she said. "He's always saying if I want to stop I should stop. I mean he's not trying to get me to play tennis, he's giving me the fun to play. He's doing everything so that I should have fun."

Philip de Picciotto, Graf's agent, agreed. "The big thing about the Grafs is that Steffi gets along so well with her father. . . . They really share a common goal and that's why they get along so well."

Peter convinced Steffi to take three months off at the end of 1985. He didn't want her to get tired of tennis. "My father makes sure I do not play too much," she explained later. "It's tough keeping my hands off a racket. During my time off, there are three and a half hours a day with nothing to do. After a week I go crazy."

While she was resting, Steffi heard the news that she was now the sixth-ranked woman in the world, behind Navratilova, Chris Evert, Hana Mandlikova, Shriver, and Claudia Kohde-Kilsch. Before she began competing she resumed practice. During a few weeks under the watchful eye of her father, she improved her game by learning a new shot—the topspin backhand.

When she came back, Graf met Evert in the finals of the

1986 Family Circle Magazine Cup. Both players stayed near the baseline, driving the ball back and forth at each other. Steffi won 6–4, 7–5. "It was nice that Steffi won her first tournament," Evert said. "Unfortunately, it was against me."

A week later Graf won again, beating Kohde-Kilsch, 6–4, 5–7, 7–6, for the Sunkist Championship. But that victory was overshadowed by a penalty against Steffi. The officials said her father had been coaching her from the stands with hand signals. That's illegal, and Graf had a point taken from her score. Steffi was angry. "He was cheering me on and, through your emotion, you move your hands," she said. "I didn't recognize any signal." But other players said there was no doubt they were cheating. "If you're an opponent, playing by the rules, that kind of thing can be difficult to accept," Evert said. "It's just not fair."

At the 1986 German Open, Steffi faced Navratilova. In their three previous meetings, Graf hadn't even won a set. This time was different. Steffi used her power to slam the ball past Martina again and again. When it was over, Navratilova was in tears and Graf had a 6–2, 6–3 victory. "It was an execution," Martina said.

But then Steffi ran into some bad luck. She caught a virus that kept her out of Wimbledon. And at the Federation Cup Tournament in Prague, Czechoslovakia, a big sun umbrella was tipped over by the wind and crashed onto her foot. Her big toe was broken. It looked as if she'd have to sit out the rest of the year.

But Steffi wasn't about to quit. She had a special oversized tennis shoe made so that she could play with a cast on her toe. Just before the U.S. Open, she won a tournament in Mahwah, New Jersey. Then at the Open she battled her way into the finals against Navratilova. The first set was interrupted by rain, and Martina won easily, 6–1. In the

After mastering the topspin backhand, Steffi began winning more tournaments.

second, she was ahead, 4–2, before Steffi managed to tie it, 6–6, then win the tiebreaker.

The third set also had to be decided by a tiebreaker. The set and the match couldn't end until a player had won by two points. Martina and Steffi were both playing so well that it appeared the match might never end. With the score 8–8, Steffi rushed to the net and missed the ball. Navratilova held a finger in the air. She needed just one more point. When Graf returned the next serve into the net, the match was finally over.

Tennis Magazine called it the Match of the Year. Fans said Steffi was now almost as good as Navratilova and Evert, who had been the two top-ranked players almost continually since 1975. But Steffi wasn't pleased. She didn't want to be almost as good as anybody—she wanted to be Number One in the world.

In November, Navratilova beat Graf again, this time in the finals of the season-ending championships in New York City. Steffi and her father decided it was again time for a rest. She told reporters that afterward she was going to work on her serve, her backhand, and her net game—back home in Germany. Actually, during this rest period Steffi didn't do much resting. She ran, lifted weights, and even jumped rope with weights on her ankles. She also spent several hours a day on the court, practicing with her father and Pavel Slozil, a former Czechoslovakian tennis champion who was now her hitting coach.

Graf ended 1986 ranked third in the world, behind Navratilova and Evert. She had yet to win any Grand Slam tournaments, but her victories had earned her $612,118. That was not what interested her, though. "If I win, the money will come. I don't like to spend money too much." Soon, she hoped, she would be the best player in the world.

Graf won her first tournament in 1986 by beating tennis champion Chris Evert.

Her opponents saw the new, improved Graf at the Lipton Players Championships in Key Biscayne, Florida, in March 1987. In her first five matches, Steffi won ten straight sets, losing only twelve games. After being destroyed 6–0, 6–1 in just thirty-six minutes, Lisa Bonder said, "I've played Martina. I've played Chris. Nobody hits the ball as hard as Steffi does."

Then Graf demolished Navratilova, 6–3, 6–2. "There's no two ways about it, she outplayed me," Martina said. "Today she was the best player in the world."

Evert was her next victim, and she lasted only fifty-eight minutes, 6–1, 6–2. "Steffi plays like she's in a hurry," Chris said. "It's sort of like she wants to get off the court." Graf acted as if she couldn't believe it. "I'm surprised by how easily I won. I thought it would be a much tougher match."

Now the stage seemed to be set for a great new player to take over the top spot. Steffi was playing the best tennis of her career. She had defeated the best players in the world. She couldn't wait to start winning Grand Slam events. Nobody asked her any more if she was sorry she had decided to take up tennis as a career. During a brief trip home to Bruhl, she smiled when she thought about what the future would bring. "Golly," she said, "I have a great life for seventeen, don't I? Everyone would choose my life, wouldn't they?"

Chapter 4

Early in 1987, Steffi Graf passed Chris Evert in the women's tennis rankings. Now only Martina Navratilova stood between her and the Number One spot. For five years, Martina had been on top of the sports world. Even though Steffi was only seventeen, her goal was to take Navratilova's place.

She won the Family Circle Magazine Cup and the Women's Tennis Association Championships (WTA), two tournaments in which Navratilova did not play. Then, after a slow start, she beat Gabriela Sabatini, 7–5, 4–6, 6–0, in the finals of the Italian Open. While she was competing there, several Italian newspapers made fun of her looks. Steffi didn't think that was funny. She said she would never play in the Italian Open again. Soon she was back home in Germany, where she took the German Open in Berlin.

By then she had won six straight tournaments. Finally it was time to face Navratilova in the French Open, Steffi's first Grand Slam event of 1987. She was confident. "I used to be a little bit scared of Chris and Martina," she said. "Now it's their turn to be scared of me."

As expected, she and Navratilova met in the championship match. Graf took the first set, 6–4, but then lost, 4–6. Martina seized the lead in the deciding third set and was a point away from the title. But then she surprised everybody in the arena by missing two straight serves. A few minutes later Navratilova was again serving for the match, and once again double faulted. That mistake seemed to take the wind out of her sails. Graf hung on to win the third set, 8–6. It was her first Grand Slam title. At seventeen she was the youngest champion in the history of the French Open.

Winning her first really big tournament was nice, but now Steffi set her sights on Wimbledon, the biggest prize of all. For more than a hundred years, great players had competed on the grass courts of the All England Lawn Tennis and Racquet Club near London. In the stands, kings and queens joined celebrities from around the world. It was the most prestigious tournament in tennis, and Navratilova was its dominant competitor. Since 1978, she had played in seven Wimbledon finals—and had won them all. Going into 1987, she had five titles in a row.

Steffi had never made it to the finals. Also, she didn't have much experience on grass courts. In fact, she hadn't played on one in two years. But none of that bothered Graf. She was determined to be the player who finally beat Martina at Wimbledon. She skipped another tournament so that she could get in some extra practice before competition began at the All England Club, midway through June.

During these practice sessions, Steffi concentrated on strengthening her serve. That was painfully obvious to Adriana Villagran, the opponent she defeated in the opening round, 6–0, 6–2. She looked unstoppable as she worked her way through the tournament. In the last semifinals, she

Steffi struggles to hit a forehand. In the 1987 French Open, she narrowly defeated Navratilova, making her the youngest champion in the history of the tournament.

crushed Pam Shriver, 6–0, 6–2, in a match that lasted only fifty-one minutes.

Other players were impressed. "I can't believe how hard Steffi hits the ball," said Evert.

Billie Jean King agreed. "She's wonderful. Steffi always had better footwork than the other kids, more discipline, and she quite frankly liked the pressure."

And what could be more pressure-packed than a final match against Navratilova on the center court at Wimbledon? Many fans thought Steffi, who had just turned eighteen, was the woman who could finally take away Martina's crown. After all, the veteran was already thirty years old. Tennis was supposed to be a young woman's game.

But besides being a gifted athlete, Navratilova was one of the cleverest players ever to pick up a racket. She knew Graf had one of the most powerful forehand shots in tennis. She also knew that was a shot she didn't want to see much. So Martina consistently hit to the other side, forcing Steffi to use her backhand. She sliced her serves near the sidelines so Steffi would have to run for the ball. She could never get her feet set for that powerful forehand return.

The strategy worked. Graf's power didn't do her any good because she never got a chance to use it. Navratilova managed to control the action, and won in straight sets, 7–5, 6–3. It was her sixth straight Wimbledon title—nobody else had ever won more than five in a row. The loss was Steffi's first in 1987.

Graf was disappointed, but she knew she would soon get another shot at the champ. In the meantime, she led West Germany into the Federation Cup team championship against the United States. In the singles final, she beat Evert, 6–2, 6–1. In the doubles final, she and her partner, Claudia Kohde-Kilsch, dropped the first set to Evert and Shriver, 1–6.

In her first appearance in a Wimbledon final, Graf was defeated by Navratilova. Martina consistently hit the ball down the line, forcing Steffi to keep running the whole match.

Steffi crushes the ball with a forehand, her most powerful stroke.

But then they rallied to win the next two sets and clinch West Germany's first Federation Cup title.

A few weeks later, on August 17, 1987, Graf beat Evert again, this time at a tournament in Los Angeles. As the match ended, Peter stood up in the stands and gave her a thumbs-up sign. At first she didn't realize what his signal meant. Then she understood and smiled. Her father was telling her that she was now the Number One player in the world.

Tennis rankings are a complex system of average points earned by match wins and tournament titles. Steffi's victory over Evert had pushed her into the top spot. When she finally got to her father, she told him, "It's time to go to the beach." So Peter, Steffi, and her brother Michael went to nearby Manhattan Beach. Her celebration was a fast run on the sand. "I'll never forget that feeling," she said.

And so, even though Steffi had only beaten Navratilova once in 1987, she was still officially the best professional women's player in the world. But Navratilova knew that all the statistics and rankings wouldn't help Steffi when she stepped onto the court. To be recognized by the fans as the best player in the world, Graf had to beat Martina.

The two great stars met again in September at the final match of the U.S. Open. Once again Navratilova concentrated on hitting the ball to Graf's backhand. And she surprised Steffi by continually rushing forward and playing close to the net. Once again her strategy worked, and she defeated Steffi, 7–6, 6–1.

But Graf still had enough wins to stay on top of the complicated rankings system. Then in the season-ending championships in November, she had trouble in the final match against Sabatini. After losing the first set, 4–6, she bounced back to win the next three, 6–4, 6–0, 6–4, and take the best-of-five match. After that Steffi and her father went home to Germany for several weeks of rest.

It had been quite a year. She earned $1,063,785 in 1987. Of thirteen tournaments she entered, she won eleven. Of the seventy-two matches she played, she won seventy. But the tournaments she lost, Wimbledon and the U.S. Open, were two of the most important. And the only person who had beaten her was Martina Navratilova, who had won two of their three matches.

Graf might be the highest-ranked player in the world, but many fans wondered if she was really the best. In order to convince them, she still had to beat Navratilova.

Chapter 5

After 1988, there were no more doubters. "When Steffi Graf became Number One, she just left everyone in the dust," said Gene Beckwith, the mathematics expert who kept track of the women's rankings. On her way to the Grand Slam, Steffi beat Chris Evert at the Australian Open, Natalia Zvereva at the French Open, Martina Navratilova at Wimbledon, and Gabriela Sabatini at the U.S. Open. A few days later she took the Olympic gold medal by defeating Zina Garrison, to complete the "Golden Slam."

Graf looked just as tough in 1989. At the Australian Open, she didn't lose a set the entire tournament. When she beat Helena Sukova in the finals, it was her fifth Grand Slam title in a row. After losing a lopsided match to Graf in Florida, Helen Kelesi said, "It was scary out there. I was just trying to hit the ball back, and I couldn't even do that.

Steffi's forehand shot was still her most powerful weapon. "There's nobody else in the world who can do what she does," Garrison said. "She's just total power. Her forehand puts fear in everybody."

Graf has become so successful that some call her a "winning machine."

Terry Phelps said she was an incredible competitor. "She doesn't like to lose a single point. She's always like that, so intense. For two years she's been like that. You'd think after a while she'd get bored."

Steffi wasn't ever bored, but sometimes she was tired of working so hard. There never seemed to be time for anything but tennis. "Tennis courts and always the same cities," she said. "But I never get to see the Rocky Mountains, for instance, or Niagara Falls." When she saw the Broadway musical *Phantom of the Opera,* she had to go back to her hotel at intermission because she had a match the next day. When her brother Michael took a vacation in Hawaii, she had to stay in Florida. "It's not fair," she said. "He's going to Hawaii, and I have to stay here and practice. I've never even been to Hawaii. But I keep telling myself the fun times will come later."

Graf continued to destroy her opponents until she ran into Arantxa Sanchez Vicario in the finals of the 1989 French Open. Before then Sanchez Vicario had never won so much as a set against Steffi, but that day she played the match of her life. "She was making some unbelievable shots," Graf said. "So close to the lines. I was not the one who was putting pressure on . . . today." Arantxa won, 7–6, 3–6, 7–5, and Steffi's Grand Slam streak was over.

The two players met again in the quarterfinals at Wimbledon, and this time Graf won 7–5, 6–1. Then, after dropping Evert, 6–2, 6–1, she beat Navratilova, 6–2, 6–7, 6–1. Martina won the first set at the U.S. Open final, but Steffi rallied to win the match, 3–6, 7–5, 6–1. A reporter asked, "Do you like being labeled a machine?" She replied, "I am a machine." A winning machine.

Graf took the 1990 Australian Open, her third in a row, by beating Mary Joe Fernandez, 6–3, 6–4. But then early in

45

February, she decided to relax by going skiing at St. Moritz, Switzerland. Even in her parka, she was a very recognizable figure. Several photographers chased her around the slopes, trying for pictures. Attempting to get away from them, she slipped and fell. She broke her right thumb, an injury that kept her out of action for two months.

But when she returned to the Bausch & Lomb Championships in Amelia Island, Florida, the thumb didn't seem to bother her at all. It only took her forty-seven minutes to whip Sanchez Vicario, 6–1, 6–0. "The way she plays today, nobody could've beaten her," Arantxa said. "Every time I hit what I think is a winner she hits it back harder."

Steffi took time out from tennis to pose for a fashion photographer. She still remembered the nasty remarks made about her looks in an article two years before and she wanted her fans to see what she really looked like. That is, when she wasn't wearing a ponytail and chasing a tennis ball. Suddenly it was obvious that Steffi was a beautiful young woman. One of the photos appeared on the cover of *Bunte,* a German magazine—in it, Graf wore high heels and a short black dress. It was one of the magazine's most popular issues ever.

She was surprised by the reaction to the photographs. "First people say, 'How's your thumb?' The next thing they say is, 'Great modeling!' Even when I won the Grand Slam, I didn't get so many congratulations." It seemed strange that people paid more attention to a few photographs than to her tennis accomplishments.

Steffi herself was becoming an accomplished photographer. When she was off the court, she said she always took her camera. "Mostly I like to take photographs of people. And I love New York City for photography because you see places or things that you rarely see. Not even always the nice photos, but some ugly ones like wrecked cars or trash cans."

Most of the time, of course, she wasn't taking pictures. People were taking pictures of her. Every place she went she was chased by photographers and reporters. Then, during the 1990 German Open, reporters discovered that a young woman was trying to blackmail Peter Graf. She said that he was the father of her baby. Eventually he was able to prove the story wasn't true, but by then Steffi was very tired of being asked about it. She felt the reporters were trying to break up her family. She said she was considering leaving Germany "if the newspapers continue to hurt me and my family with their headlines."

She was so upset that she fled into a forest. "There, I ran alone through the woods, sat down somewhere and thought: 'Steffi, you have to rise above this.' Yet after I returned to my hotel, I still was so deeply hurt that I asked myself: 'How can I go on with this tournament?'"

At the German Open she found it very hard to keep her mind on tennis. "I played without concentrating," she said. "That leads to a loss of self-confidence, of course, and to the loss of matches." In the final match, she lost to Monica Seles, a sixteen-year-old Yugoslavian who grunted every time she hit the ball. Reporters said she laughed like the cartoon character Woody Woodpecker. Graf found nothing to laugh about. After losing, she smashed a hole in the locker room wall with her racket. Then a few weeks later she lost the French Open title to Seles, 7–6, 6–4. At Wimbledon, she didn't even make it to the final. She was defeated in the semi-finals by Zina Garrison-Jackson, who had changed her name after her recent marriage. Tennis fans wondered if Graf was finished. Was she a twenty-one-year-old has-been? Steffi tried to act as if it wasn't important. "It's just a simple loss," she said at Wimbledon. "What else [do] you think? A tragedy? A disaster?"

Graf smashes a crosscourt backhand.

Things didn't get any better at the U.S. Open, where she lost the final to Gabriela Sabatini. After the Grand Slam in 1988, everything seemed to be going downhill. She had only one major tournament victory in 1990, but she still had enough wins to stay on top of the rankings. Right behind her were Seles and Navratilova.

Graf didn't play really strong tennis again until the early rounds of a tournament in Boca Raton, Florida, in March 1991. After polishing off Nathalie Tauziat in the semifinals, 6–1, 6–2, she said, "It's a relief just to play this way." But then in the next match she was defeated by Sabatini, 6–4, 7–6. "She knows she's losing the Number One and she's losing confidence," the winner said. "It's different when you are Number One and you feel it. I don't think she's feeling it." In fact, after her loss to Sabatini, Graf was no longer the top-ranked player in the world. After 186 weeks on top, she was now Number Two.

The new leader was Seles, the seventeen-year-old who was earning a reputation as a tough competitor. "She patrolled the baseline like a guard dog assigned to enemy territory," was how one columnist described her game.

"I don't understand the ranking system at all," Seles said. "But I know I deserve it." She celebrated with a big party at a club in Sarasota, Florida, saying, "This feeling will only happen once."

Steffi wondered if she would ever have that Number One feeling again. She didn't have much to say to reporters. "I care about losing, not the Number One ranking," she told them. Then she did what she always did after a disappointing day on the courts. "After a loss," she said, "I always go to bed very, very early." She slept it off and waited for the chance to put her career back together.

Chapter 6

The 1991 French Open was a disaster for Steffi Graf. In her semifinal match with Arantxa Sanchez Vicario, she couldn't seem to keep the ball in the court, and her forehand had no zip at all. She lost the first set, 6–0. It was the first time in seven years that she had lost a love set.

Up in the stands, Steffi's father had jumped out of his seat to punch a fan. Mr. Graf then tried to leave, but the fan hit him in the back and shouted, "Wait until Wimbledon! I'll have a bodyguard and he'll break Peter's legs!" Later Steffi's father claimed the fan had been irritating their family for years.

Back on the court, Steffi's miserable performance continued. Sanchez Vicario easily won the second set, 6–2. The entire match had taken just forty-three minutes. "I've never felt such a sense of powerlessness," Graf said. "I can't remember when I played that badly. . . . And Arantxa was hitting incredible shots." Graf was angry when reporters asked about her father's fight in the stands. "I don't know what happened and I don't care!" When Monica Seles beat Sanchez

With the increasing pressures of stardom, and stiffer competition from players such as Arantxa Sanchez Vicario and Monica Seles, Steffi slipped from the Number One spot.

Vicario in the final, 6–3, 6–4, she strengthened her hold on the Number One spot.

The leg-breaking bodyguard didn't show up at Wimbledon. But neither did Seles. Without giving a reason, she withdrew from the tournament and disappeared. Tennis officials couldn't find her to ask her why. "She thinks she's Madonna," said a disgusted player. Why would the world's top-ranked player skip the world's most important tournament? Nobody knew.

Steffi tried to forget the controversies about her father's fight and Monica's absence, and concentrate on her tennis. She made it to the final against Gabriela Sabatini, who had beaten her five times in a row. And nobody had to remind Graf that she hadn't won a Grand Slam event in eighteen months.

Steffi won the first set, 6–4, then dropped the second, 3–6. The third set was tied, 4–4, when Graf seemed to lose her concentration. She hit an easy forehand far out of bounds and double faulted twice to lose the game. Gabriela needed just one more game to take the championship, but she couldn't win her serve, either, and it was tied again at 5–5. Steffi then continued her sloppy play by losing her serve when she hit a forehand shot into the net.

Once again Sabatini needed just one more game. When it was tied at 30–30, both players rushed the net. Steffi tried to lob a shot over Gabriela's head, but she managed to return it by jumping high in the air. Unfortunately, as she said later, "I just put it right in the middle, an easy ball for her." Graf slapped the ball back for a point, then tied the set, 6–6, with a forehand shot that Sabatini couldn't reach.

After that, Gabriela seemed to run out of gas. When Steffi finally won the match two games later by slashing back Sabatini's serve, she leaned back and screamed for joy. "I

Monica Seles was Steffi's toughest competitor until Monica was stabbed by a fan during a match in Germany.

needed this," she said. "It pulled me out of a low. That victory was so important for my self-confidence."

The win at Wimbledon wasn't enough for Graf to regain the Number One ranking. A month later she was on top briefly when Seles lost a tournament to Jennifer Capriati. Then in the semifinals of the 1991 U.S. Open, Steffi lost to Martina Navratilova, who hadn't beaten her in four years. When Seles defeated Navratilova, 7–6, 6–1, for the title, Monica was back on top. When reporters told her she was Number One again, she said, "Oh, I forgot about that."

Nobody could accuse Steffi of forgetting about the rankings. For the next eighteen months she couldn't take the Number One spot back from Seles. What was wrong? Was Monica really a better player? "Graf is the best athlete on the tour, but mentally Seles is by far the strongest," said Tom Gullikson, then Capriati's coach. Steffi's former coach, Pavel Slozil, agreed. "In my heart Steffi's still Number One," he said. "I think she's a better player than Seles, but she's not as confident, which is why Seles is racking up Grand Slam after Grand Slam."

Many people blamed Graf's troubles on her father. They said she would be a better player if she didn't always have to worry about him. She admitted all the newspaper stories upset her, and blamed that on the reporters. But she felt her biggest problem was that "I'm playing badly, get mad at myself and thus pull myself farther and farther down." She also said, "I used to be stronger, probably, much calmer and much, much more self-confident than I am now."

She tried to relax by playing pinball and racing down country roads in her Porsche sports car. If that didn't work, she enjoyed piloting a helicopter. Reporters said she ran the cars and the copters the same way she played tennis—at top speed. They also followed her around when she tried to play with her dogs, Enzo, Max, and Ben. Because she was so popular in Germany, somebody seemed always to be after her—fans, reporters, or photographers. She and her family began spending most of their time at their second home in Florida.

Steffi wished she had more privacy, but she knew she was a lucky young woman. How many people in their early twenties were millionaires? She was making a fortune playing tennis and endorsing products like Adidas shoes, Dunlop rackets, and Opel automobiles. It was a good life—but it would be a lot more fun if she were winning more.

Steffi wasn't the only player the reporters were after. During the 1992 Wimbledon tournament, newspapers were full of comments about the strange noises Seles made on the court. Ever since she began playing professional tennis, she had grunted every time she hit the ball. "It's part of my game," she said. "I hate it. I can't help it." One newspaper article said she sounded like "strangled bagpipes" or "feeding time at the zoo."

Navratilova was tired of Seles's noise. She said the grunts made it impossible to hear her racket hit the ball. Worse yet, she claimed, Monica sometimes yelled the loudest when she was hitting the ball softly. In their semifinal match, Martina complained to the umpire, "She sounds like a stuck pig!" But Seles kept grunting and won easily, 6–2, 6–4.

In the final against Graf, though, Seles was silent. For the first time, she played a match and didn't grunt. Without the sound effects, she was no match for Steffi. "Whatever I tried, they kept not going there," she said after losing, 6–2, 6–1. It was the first time she had ever lost a Grand Slam final. Graf was surprised to finish off her rival in just fifty-eight minutes, but she said, "I knew I had it in me."

Except for Wimbledon, Steffi didn't win any major tournaments in 1992. She was even defeated in the Olympic gold medal match by Capriati, a sixteen-year-old who had never beaten her before.

Graf began 1993 by winning the first set of the Australian Open final, 6–4, against Seles, before dropping the next two and the title. Monica remained comfortably on top of the rankings.

Then, during a changeover in a match in Hamburg, Germany, Seles was stabbed in the back by a fan. The knife barely missed her spinal cord, and she was carried bleeding from the court. The man hadn't tried to kill her, a police spokesman announced. "He only wanted to injure her so Steffi Graf could become Number One again."

Graf was, of course, shocked. She didn't have to tell anybody that she had wanted to regain the top spot by beating Seles. Not *this* way.

At the French Open final a few weeks later, with Monica out of action, Steffi beat Mary Joe Fernandez, 4–6, 6–2, 6–4. By the time of the Wimbledon tournament in June, it was obvious that it would take Seles months to recover from the stabbing. Then Steffi herself received a threat, and felt she must hire a bodyguard. Besides that, she was still upset about the attack on Seles. And she developed a sore right foot. Some fans didn't think she would last long at Wimbledon.

Steffi made it to the final against Jana Novotna. She managed to win the first set, 7–6, but dropped the second, 1–6. Novotna kept bringing Graf to the net with short shots, then lobbing the ball over her head or blasting it down the sidelines. She sailed to a 4–1 lead in the final, deciding set and was serving a 40–30 lead. Novotna was just a point and a game away from the most important championship in tennis. Then she cracked.

She gave away her serve with three terrible shots, then lost the next two games. Steffi couldn't believe her good luck. The set was tied, 4–4. Jana got only one point in the next two games, and the title belonged to Graf. It was her third straight Wimbledon championship and the fifth in six years.

After the match, Novotna congratulated Graf, but began crying when she accepted her runner-up plate. Tears filled Steffi's eyes, too. "Once I saw her face, I knew exactly what was going through her mind. I really felt bad."

Still unable to play, Monica Seles continued to make news in September at the U.S. Open. She told reporters she was surprised Steffi hadn't gotten in touch with her after the stabbing. Apparently she had forgotten that Graf visited her at the hospital in Hamburg. Steffi had also tried to talk to her during the summer. "It's just impossible to reach her," she said. Sometimes Monica's agents couldn't even find her.

Back on the court, Graf was once again playing great tennis. "She's more independent, and it shows in her tennis," said her coach, Heinz Gunthardt. She seemed to be making more decisions on her own, without relying on her father for advice. And she had moved into her own penthouse apartment in New York City. "To have a place of my own, to be able to decorate it myself, it's something I've always wished for."

Steffi also had a boyfriend, Peter Michael Bartels, a twenty-five-year-old German race car driver. When a fan yelled "I love you, Steffi!" she smiled and said, "I'm taken."

She ran over the competition at the U.S. Open, beating Helena Sukova in the final, 6–3, 6–3. It was her thirty-sixth match victory in a row and her sixth straight title. If she hadn't lost to Seles in the Australian Open, she would have had her second Grand Slam.

Graf was once more on top of the tennis world. By the time she won the Virginia Slims Championship against Sanchez Vicario in November, she had earned $2,753,000 in 1993 alone. That gave her career earnings of more than thirteen million dollars. "I'm incredibly happy to end the year like this," she said. "It couldn't be any better."

But some fans complained that Steffi was winning too

easily simply because she didn't have enough competition. Seles was still recovering from the stabbing, and Capriati had given up tennis to return to high school. Then Navratilova and Garrison-Jackson announced they would both retire at the end of 1994. Graf was as anxious as the fans to see tougher competition. Seles, she said, "played her part in motivating me and making me a better player. Since she went, my victories have never really been accepted by the public. I wish Monica and Jennifer would both return."

Early in 1994, Steffi destroyed Arantxa Sanchez Vicario at the finals of the Australian Open in just fifty-eight minutes. She never lost a set in the entire tournament. The victory in Australia gave her four Grand Slam championships in a row.

But then at the semifinals of the French Open, Steffi played Mary Pierce, a nineteen-year-old American. Almost everybody expected another easy Graf win, but Pierce took a quick 6–2, 6–2 victory. "I'm a little shocked at the way I won so easily," she said."I felt there wasn't much that she could do because I was just playing so well."

Steffi agreed. "She attacked the ball, took the ball early and played very deep. There was very little I could do."

Despite a disappointing first round loss on Wimbledon's grass courts, she seemed to be invincible. In fact, she never lost a match in 1994 on hardcourt until Sanchez Vicario beat her, 7–5, 1–6, 7–6, in the finals of the Matinee International Tournament in August.

From there, Graf cruised through the opening rounds of the U.S. Open. But then she again ran into Arantxa in the final. After taking an easy 6–1 first set victory, Steffi's back began giving her trouble. She tried stretching to lessen the pain, but the longer the match went on the worse her back felt. Sanchez Vicario won the last two sets and the title, 7–6, 6–4.

But Graf refused to blame the loss on her bad back: "All

Graf holds up the championship trophy after winning the 1994 Australian Open.

I'm going to say . . . Arantxa was just better today." Two months later her back was still sore, and her doctor said it might even require surgery.

By the end of 1994, Steffi Graf was still only twenty-five years old, but she had been playing professional tennis for twelve years. As soon as her back felt better, she wanted to be back out on the court.

"I am more prone to injuries," she said. "First it was the shoulder, then the foot, next the back, and in between, a bone infection in my hand." She didn't enjoy the constant attention of her fans and the press. "Everything I do gets noticed and I just wish it wasn't like that."

But she still tried to focus her attention on the game she loved. "I have only one aim," she said. "To fulfill my potential. When I lose a match, I realize there is still a lot missing."

Of course, she realized there was a lot more to life than tennis. "I have tried to build three lives," she said. "There is my family, my tennis and my private life, which I am enjoying so much these days. Right now, I'd say I was very happy."

Career Statistics

SINGLES

Year	Tournaments							Matches			
	Tot	W	F	S	Q	E	Qa	Tot	W	L	Pct.
1982	1	0	0	0	0	1	0	1	0	1	0.000
1983	15	0	0	1	1	9	4	36	21	15	0.583
1984	14	0	1	0	1	11	1	33	19	14	0.576
1985	13	0	3	4	1	5	0	53	40	13	0.755
1986	15	8	3	2	1	0	1	70	64	6	0.914
1987	13	11	2	0	0	0	0	77	75	2	0.974
1988	14	11	1	2	0	0	0	75	72	3	0.960
1989†	16	14	2	0	0	0	1	88	86	2	0.977
1990	15	10	3	2	0	0	0	77	72	5	0.935
1991†	15	7	2	3	3	0	1	73	65	8	0.890
1992†	15	8	3	2	1	1	1	78	71	7	0.910
1993†	15	10	4	1	0	0	1	82	76	6	0.926
1994	12	7	3	1	0	1	0	62	57	5	0.919
Total	173	86	27	18	8	28	10	805	718	87	0.891

Tot=Total, W=Win, F=Final, S=Semifinal, Q=Quarterfinal, E=Eliminated earlier, Qa=Qualified, L=Loss, Pct.=Percentage
†=Totals do not include Federation Cup.

GRAND SLAM WINS (singles)	
Tournament	Years Won
U.S. Open	1988*, 1989, 1993
French Open	1987, 1988*, 1993
Australian Open	1988*, 1989, 1990, 1994
Wimbledon	1988*, 1989, 1991, 1992, 1993

*Grand Slam

DOUBLES

	Tournaments						Matches			
Year	Tot	W	F	S	Q	E	Qa	Tot	W	L	Pct.
1983	2	0	0	0	0	2	0	2	0	2	0.000
1984	10	0	0	0	0	10	0	15	5	10	0.333
1985	14	0	1	1	4	8	0	29	15	14	0.517
1986	13	5	4	2	0	2	0	53	45	8	0.849
1987	10	1	1	3	1	3	1	30	24	6	0.800
1988	7	2	0	5	0	0	0	31	26	5	0.839
1989	8	1	1	2	2	2	0	29	23	6	0.793
1990	4	0	0	0	2	2	0	10	7	3	0.700
1991†	2	0	0	0	1	1	1	4	2	2	0.500
1992†	6	1	0	2	1	2	1	19	14	5	0.736
1993	2	1	0	0	1	0	0	6	6	0	1.000
1994	3	0	0	0	0	3	0	5	2	3	0.400
Total	79	11	7	15	12	35	3	233	169	64	0.725

†=Totals do not include Federation Cup.

Where to Write Steffi Graf

Ms. Steffi Graf
c/o W.T.A. Tour Players Association
133 First St., N.E.
St. Petersburg, FL 33701

Index